Friends and Enemies

Friends and Enemies

A book of short prayers & some ways to write your own

Ruth Burgess

WILD GOOSE PUBLICATIONS

Prayers © the individual contributors
Compilation and workshops © 2003 Ruth Burgess

First published 2004 by

Wild Goose Publications, 4th Floor, Savoy House, 140 Sauchiehall St, Glasgow G2 3DH, UK.
Wild Goose Publications is the publishing division of the Iona Community.
Scottish Charity No. SCO03794. Limited Company Reg. No. SCO96243.
www.ionabooks.com

ISBN 1 901557 78 2

Cover illustration from the painting 'Urban Spirit' © Jocelyn Prosser
www.artnaive.co.uk

The publishers gratefully acknowledge the support of the Drummond Trust,
3 Pitt Terrace, Stirling FK8 2EY in producing this book.

Overseas distribution:
Australia: Willow Connection Pty Ltd, Unit 4A, 3-9 Kenneth Road, Manly Vale, NSW 2093
New Zealand: Pleroma, Higginson Street, Otane 4170, Central Hawkes Bay
Canada: Novalis Publishing & Distribution, 49 Front Street East, Toronto, Ontario M5E 1B3

Permission to reproduce any part of this work in Australia or New Zealand should be
sought from Willow Connection.

Printed by Bell & Bain, Thornliebank, Glasgow

For Eve, Mona, Ruth, Vera, Isobel, Mabel and Enid
storytellers, nurturers, adventurers,
wise women on my track

and for Ian and Ian
wise men of integrity, laughter and hope

with thanks for your courage and love

Contents

Index of titles

The daily silencing – prayers of (those labelled) enemies   43

Neighbours and communities   51

Introduction

This book brings together prayers about friends, enemies and relationships. There are also prayers pertaining to daily life and to particular moments and places.

Most of the prayers are written in inclusive language, although for some writers exclusive words still have a positive and significant meaning in their relationship with God. Neither our use of language nor our relationship with God is static; God-words and the words of our prayers will always be fluid.

There are strong thoughts and words in some of these prayers. Saying what we mean to God is more honest than tiptoeing around the issues and concerns we find disturbing or difficult. To write with integrity is to write within the traditions of the writers of the psalms. There is also much wisdom and humour in these prayers, and the challenging clarity of children's conversations with God.

There are three prayer-writing workshops included in this book. These are based on experience of working with groups to write poems and prayers for private and public use:

- A Haiku Prayer Workshop is an introduction to short prayer writing, which can be enjoyed by participants of all ages.
- Writing Personal Prayers is an experimental workshop encouraging creativity and reflection.
- A Workshop on Writing Intercessory/Bidding Prayers is included, as these are the prayers that lay people are most often asked to contribute to public worship.

My thanks are due to all the contributors who wrote prayers for this book. I also want to thank Lindsay Gray, Jan Sutch Pickard and class teachers who encouraged children to write; Bernadette and Peter Askins and Linda and David Bosworth for proof reading; and Yvonne Morland for sharing with me her experience of running creative writing workshops. I am grateful to the Wild Goose Publications team: Sandra, Jane, Neil, Alex and Tri, for all their encouragement, professionalism and support.

I have greatly enjoyed compiling and editing this book. I hope it will be a useful prayer and worship resource, and an encouragement to both individuals and congregations to be creative and courageous in their prayers.

Friends

Today and tomorrow

Give us bread and friends today,
seeds and stories tomorrow,
love and laughter
for ever and ever.

Joy Mead

Companions on the road

God, we thank you
for the companionship of friends,
and for encounters with strangers;
and the discovery that there are other folk –
saints and sinners like ourselves –
willing to follow you. Amen

Jan Sutch Pickard

Friendship

God, friend and lover of all,
thank you for the wonders of friendship.
For exasperation and encouragement,
irritation and delight,
earthy laughter and shared tears;

and the sheer taking-for-granted of a friend's presence
in daily routine and sudden crisis.

God, friend and lover of all,
help me, humbly and gladly,
to offer my presence
in friendship to your creation.

Jan Berry

Friends underestimated

Lord of surprises, humble us with friendship

– a perceptive word out of the blue
– an unexpected arm around the shoulder
– a vivid flash of anger on our behalf.

It is here that your kingdom comes.

Nick Burden

Friends

Friends demand the real you,
not the edited version.
They don't fuss when you stagger and sway,
understanding that we all have the right to stand on our own two feet
and fall flat on our faces sometimes.
They trust you to ask for help when it's needed,
but don't impose it.
They share laughter with you,
grumbles too,
and dare to look you in the eye,
even though you mirror their own mortality,
their own uncertainty.
How should they know how to react to you
when often you don't know how to react to yourself?
Friends share the way with you
and the muddle too.
That's love.

Frances Copsey

The bestest friend

Dear God,
You are the bestest friend I have got, then my mum.
Please help us.
You're my friend.

Michelle (Aged 8)

Thank you for old friends #1

God, thank you for the old friends I turn to when I am feeling alone
and crazy

Thank you for Henri Nouwen
for Vincent Van Gogh
for Sylvia Plath
for Henry David Thoreau
for William Blake
for Tennessee Williams
for Allen Ginsberg

God, thank you for the old friends I turn to when I am feeling alone
    and crazy
Old friends who restore my sanity and hope
Old friends who give me the inspiration and passion to live and love again.

Neil Paynter

Thank you for old friends #2

God, thank you for old friends I turn to when I am feeling apathetic
    and cynical

Thank you for Noam Chomsky
for Satish Kumar
for Jean Vanier
for Simone Weil
for Aung San Suu Kyi
for Bob Geldof
for Ani Pachen
for Bruce Cockburn
for Maya Angelou

God, thank you for old friends I turn to when I am feeling apathetic
    and cynical
Old friends who restore my faith and hope
Old friends who give me the energy to work for justice and peace.

Neil Paynter

Clinging on

Friends are what you cling on to
when you're at the end of your tether
and the rope's unravelling.

Frances Copsey

Thanksgiving for friends

These, these are the ones who have walked with me
where no others would come.
These are the ones who have not refused to look upon me.
These are the ones who have come near.

These are the ones who have shown me your face.
These are the ones who have touched me with your nearness.
These are the ones who have incarnated your justice.
These are the ones who have mediated your presence.

I am trembling.
I am thankful.

Nicola Slee

Blessing for friends

Your blessing be upon those
who have shared with me the gift of friendship.

Your blessing be upon those
who were once dear but with whom I have lost touch.

Your blessing be upon those
whom I find difficult,
and on those who find me difficult.

Your blessing on friends, Lord.

O God and Father of all,
in thanks for all that has been good,
in sorrow for all that has been hurtful,
I remember them.

May those whom time, distance,
death and human weakness have sundered,
be gathered up in your love,
through Jesus Christ, our Lord. Amen

Ian Cowie

Prayer for old friends who are left behind

As I step through another open door in my life,
I pray for all those friends who are left behind,
left without a key to follow
as the door falls shut.
Even if they don't understand me any longer
and we grow to be strangers in the future,
I cannot turn back.
I give thanks that they were with me on my journey
and pray that I may never forget their friendship.
May God bless and keep them safe. Amen

Jenni Sophia Fuchs

Encouragement

Bless you, my friend,
you have the gift of encouragement:
knowing intuitively where it is needed.
It is not just that you are good
at saying the right words at the right time –
but, constantly, you see the good
in each person, and you affirm it.
This is your down-to-earth ministry:
in everyday words, you do God's work.
As you are a blessing,
may you also be blessed. Amen

Jan Sutch Pickard

Christ our companion

Christ our companion,
you have given us friends
to love us, and to be loved by us.
You have travelled with us
on our varied journeys.
You have encouraged
and strengthened us
through the gift of one another,
and the beauty of creation.
Continue to be our travelling companion,
guiding us gently,
challenging us strongly,
upholding us when we fall
and nurturing us
with your presence.

Elizabeth Baxter

Old friends who understand

God, thank you for old friends

Old friends whom we may not have seen for ages
but who come to meet us where we are

Old friends who don't make us feel guilty
for not calling or sending a card, or for changing

Old friends who respect our silences,
who forgive our rants and ravings and when we talk shite

Old friends we are at home with
who are more like family
who laugh when we laugh
who cry when we cry

Old friends to whom we can confess almost anything
Old friends we can trust to be honest

Old friends who let the little things go
yet don't let us away with too much

Old friends who don't try to give answers
who know how to ask the right questions
who know how to listen

Old friends who understand
(or who try hard to understand)

Old friends
who understand us
better than we, sometimes, understand ourselves

Thank you for old friends who love us
almost as unconditionally
as you love us God.
Amen

Neil Paynter

Enemies

Two prayers for God's help

God help us to confront
the howling voices of unreason
and the chilling logic of those who deal in death.
Help us to cope
with courage, faith and cheerfulness.

O God, help us
to feel the wind of your Spirit
and to keep our feet.

Jan Sutch Pickard

Coals of fire

I rather like the idea
of heaping coals of fire
on my enemy's head, God.

It resonates with how I feel sometimes.
I suspect the psalmist felt it too –
all those passages about splattered brains
and Red Sea drownings.

Some commentaries tell me that it's really about loving my enemy,
about providing a source of heat to ignite a fire that has gone out.
But I prefer my fantasy to that.

I picture you, God, in a huge, moated castle.
Someone you don't like is approaching,
and you're sitting on the battlements
above the drawbridge
in front of a roaring fire,
poised to pull back a lever
and release burning coals on your enemies' heads!

Maybe it's me I picture on the battlements, not you.

All my experience tells me
that you are just and loving
and that you are more likely to
invite your enemies into supper
and talk with them into the night.

Blow away my fantasies, God.
Breathe your disturbing reality
into my life.
Tell me again the story of your love.

Ruth Burgess

* Proverbs 25:21–22; Romans 12:20

The man who ...

The man who blows up buses and himself
    is my brother.
The woman who ties explosives to her chest
and locks herself in a crowded theatre
    is my sister.

If I met them I'd have nothing to say.
We don't speak each other's languages
and I don't understand their culture, their passion and their beliefs.

But the man who blows up buses and himself
    is my brother.
The woman who ties explosives to her chest
and locks herself in a crowded theatre
    is my sister.

Rosie Miles

Loving enemies

You said, 'Love your enemies',
but did you mean these,
my familiar friends,
who turned on me, and betrayed me?

Maybe, in time, I will be able to forgive them
(for forgiveness does not come quickly).
But how am I supposed to eat with them,
sit with them close at my side,
pray with them,
take the bread and the cup from them,
open myself to them?
How am I supposed to look them in the eyes again,
speak peace to them,
when there is no peace?
What form can my love take
that is not a betrayal of truth?

Nicola Slee

God, I wish

God,
I wish people would leave me alone.
I wish you'd turn some into rats
so I could squash them.

Prayers from Hackwood Park School

Prayer for my enemy

May God love you
I can only hate you.

May God bless you
I can only curse you.

May God change you –
I have a few suggestions.

May God guide you
and me
into the ways of justice and peace.

Ruth Burgess

Acknowledging my enemy

I find it really hard to pray for my enemy, God.
I don't like the idea of having an 'enemy'.
I would prefer to believe that I get on with everyone
and everyone gets on with me.
But when that is not true,
help me to acknowledge
and pray for my enemy.

Margaret Harvey

Sifting the evidence

How am I to sift the evidence,
the significantly incomplete evidence,
that politicians offer me
as justification
for going to war?

And will my conclusion
make any difference
to anyone but me?

Who will listen to my thoughts?
Who cares what I think?

You care God.
You ask me
to love justice.

I will ask the questions
and weigh the evidence
and seek answers.

I will try to walk justly with
my neighbour
my enemy
and You.

Ruth Burgess

God, can you help me?

God, can you help me?
There are some people I just dislike
and find it hard to get on with,
but there are others who, frankly, I can't see any good in.

Help me to look for the good in them,
and maybe that will make me more tolerant,
and understanding of the difficulties they may face.
Help me to love them more. Amen

Jean Murdoch

Enemies within

From cynicism, contempt and indifference,
Lord, protect us.

From doubts and fears,
Lord, reassure us.

From regret for the past and dread of the future,
Lord, deliver us.

From anger and violence of hand or tongue,
Lord, restrain us.

From hypocrisy, self-importance and arrogance,
Lord, enlighten us.

From insensitivity and hardness of heart,
Lord, soften us.

Lord, teach us how to love our enemies.

Nick Burden

Prayer for friends turned enemies

Perhaps I could pray for enemies,
it would be straightforward.
They would be the ones who hate me,
who wish to do me harm.

But these: these are the ones I thought were friends.
These are the ones I have eaten with
and prayed with and laughed with.
These are the ones with whom I sat at Christ's table.

Now, without warning, they have turned from me.
They have wounded me in the deepest place of my vulnerability.
They do not speak to me; they will not look at me.

I do not know how to pray for them.
I cannot pray with them.
I only have rage and anger and pain and confusion to bear them.

God, you alone are faithful.
Accept the prayer I cannot make.

Nicola Slee

Haiku prayer of hurt

God, how do I pray
when I want to hurt those back
who keep hurting me?

Ruth Burgess

Enemies, friends

I want to live in a world where it's clear:
where enemies are enemies
and friends are the ones I can trust.

I want to live in a world where it's safe
to love and hate,
without fear of getting it wrong.

God, teach me to live with the wheat and the tares*
growing together: the wounds of friends,
the kisses of enemies.

Nicola Slee

*Matthew 13:24–30, 36–43; Proverbs 27:6

The daily silencing

– prayers of (those labelled) enemies –

The rejected one?

Dear God,
how can I ever pray this? –
the unspoken prayer of my heart.
Words of forgiveness,
easy for others to say,
but hard to bear when it's your son they killed,
your daughter crying,
you with spit on your face and worse
pushed through the letter box.
Hard to bear,
the smile of the liberal,
sure of God's grace for all,
as long as I don't raise those awkward issues:
prejudice, discrimination, racism.
On Racial Justice Sunday, we might have some special prayers
    as a concession.
Otherwise, it's so easy to see the stifled yawn,
'You people all make such as fuss.'

How do I forgive my sister and brother in Christ
for their indifference?
The one with the knife of fixed hatred is so much easier to forgive.
The rest, the passers by, so righteous in the pew –
or even in the pulpit –
I hate with a psalmist's anger for their lies that aid the racist.

Dear God,
holding me, holding them
together on the cross,
I wait, quiet now,
wanting your voice
calling me to new life.
Calling us all to let go of our selves,
to take up your cross,
to trust you in everything,
to follow you to your abandoned holding.

Dear God,
how can I ever pray this? –
the unspoken prayer of my heart.
Words of forgiveness,
easy for others to say,
but hard to bear when it's your son they killed,
your daughter crying.

Amen

Karen Reeves-Attwood

Prayer of a gay man

I do not know how to pray

    for the men who wait to beat me up when I come out of the club,
    for those who think my loving is disordered and wrong,
    for the people who pray that I may be healed,
    for the ones who wish me dead.

Help me mouth the words,
for they will not come.

Rosie Miles

Prayer of a lesbian who wishes to become a priest

God help me

in a church that takes my desire and my sense of calling,
welcomes all I give of myself and my time,
embraces my commitment to the gospel,
and which says I must never love another woman.

For if I do,
this church will rip me apart.

Rosie Miles

Remind me

Unemployed
idle
redundant
lazy
insignificant

If I listen
to the words
long enough
I become
what I am labelled

Remind me
that you love me
and respect me
God.

Ruth Burgess

What have we done?

What have we done that you cannot welcome us?
What is our crime that you do not acknowledge us?
What sin have we committed that you will not speak to us?
What horror do we bear that you will not look on us?

Our only crime was to love our own kind.
Our only sin was to demand equity.
Our only misdeed was to declare our love openly.
Our only dishonour was to hold up our heads shamelessly.

O you that judge all hearts, judge between us.
O you that welcome sinners, welcome the spurned.
O you that were among the rejected, stand with those
    who have been rejected.
O you that know all secrets, let what is hidden be disclosed.

Nicola Slee

Forgive the sin

Forgive the sin.
Forgive the policy of 'don't ask don't tell'.
Forgive the careers lost, lives damaged, callings abandoned.

Forgive the daily silencing.
Forgive the pretending we don't exist.
Forgive those who say, 'It's nothing personal,
but I can't speak out on this issue publicly.'

Forgive the fear.
Forgive the fear.
Forgive the fear.

Rosie Miles

Hungry God

Hungry God
Feed us

Lonely God
Hold us

Empty God
Fill us

Hurting God
Heal us

Silent God
Speak to us

Suffering God
Love us

Rosie Miles

Neighbours and communities

Good neighbours

Far and near,
near or far,
my neighbour
is my duty and my joy.
Her eyes are the eyes of Christ;
his hands are Christ's hands
reaching out to me
as I reach out to them.

O God, help us all to be good neighbours.[1]

Kate McIlhagga

Bread and peace

God of our open futures,
help us:

to explore
once upon a time moments
where stories begin
and outrageous hope
outspoken love
justice and joy
are released;

to see
where the nudging angels
move amongst people
longing for comfort and community
sensing beginnings of friendship
wanting touch and affirmation;

to enable
life's great feast to happen,
hearts and hands, baskets and pockets
to open,
neighbour to share bread
and peace with neighbour,
to make a place for another;

so that in the most ordinary of miracles
all are fed.

Joy Mead

May we recognise you

O Christ, may we recognise you:

in companions gathered around the table and
in colleagues meeting around the water cooler

in mysterious strangers and
in transparent family members

in next door neighbours and
in brothers and sisters across the world.

May we recognise you
in everyone we meet, O Christ.
And in all the places we share
our broken and beautiful lives.[2]

Neil Paynter

Intercession for neighbours

Lord, you commanded us to love our neighbours.
Have mercy on us for it is not easy.

Your neighbours in Nazareth tried to lynch you,
so you know our problem.

We remember before you:
good neighbours and bad neighbours;

those we know and those we do not know;
those who have problems and those who seem trouble free;
the children growing up in our midst;
older people and their needs;
our councillors and community leaders –
the whole pattern of neighbourhood life.

Lord Jesus,
you said that we are the light of the world,
so inspire us by your love
that we may do such lovely things
that our neighbours may glorify our Father in heaven.*

Ian Cowie

*Matthew 5:15–16

No one is expendable

O Lord Christ, who became poor that we might be rich,
deliver us from a comfortable conscience,
if we believe or intend that others
should be poor that we might be rich,
for in God's economy
no one is expendable.
Grant us instead the riches of love.

Kathy Galloway

One body

Jesus Christ,
you have chosen us to be a part of your body.

Some of us know our talents,
the things that we are good at.
Others often say,
'But what can I do?'

Jesus, you are wise,
and we are your choice,
and so we say *'yes'* to you
and trust your spirit to bring out the best in us.

As your body,
may we make a difference
to our church,
our community
and our world. Amen

Alison Adam

Disability

Jesus our Saviour,
you met and loved many people with disabilities,
but you saw them in a different way:
not just their condition but their capabilities,
not just what they needed but what they could give,
not just as labels but as loveable and loving people.
And the people you saw as most disabled
were the ones who could not or would not love,
and who were full of pride.
Help us to recognise where we, too, are disabled,
and to learn from those who know their need of God.

Kathy Galloway

The long loneliness

O we have all known
the long loneliness;
and now may we learn
that the only redress
is love.
And love comes from community –
the telling place of truth.
And truth heals a community –
the telling place of love.

da *Noust*

(based on some words by Dorothy Day)

2 Kings 2:23–25: The consolations of scripture
(a prayer for self-esteem – and peace among nations)

Go home baldy!
the young boys bawled.
Till prophet prayed
and bears mauled.
Dignity restored and blood spilled,
God got the blame.

Makes you feel quite good
if you can lose a hair or two
and rise above God's mouthpiece
because, despite provocation,
you let the neighbours'
kids live.

David Coleman

Carers

God, you care for us like a mother hen with her chicks,
gathering us up, sheltering us under your soft wings.
We long to trust that care, yet often draw back
afraid of our own need, afraid to let go and be loved.
Help us to let ourselves trust, let go, be loved
that we, in our turn, may love and care for others sensitively,
understand their fear of dependence,
know our own limitations, and respect theirs.

Kathy Galloway

Persevere

We persevere, a pilgrim band;
we're called –
    to live in hope, not fear,
    to welcome all we scorn or hate
    within our heart, among our kin;
a covenant of love proclaim.[3]

da *Noust*

Family

A blessing on Henry, my first grandchild

May you give and receive love.
May you trust and be trusted.
May you dare and be daring.
May you believe and be believed.
And may you live in God's sunlight all your days. Amen

Jean E.S. Williams

She who shares life with me

I give thanks for the partner who shares life with me,
who sees something in me which escapes others,
who knows my faults and still loves me,
who appreciates my strengths and gives me confidence.
I give thanks for my partner
through whom I get glimpses into your nature, Lord God.
For you, too, know me through and through and still love me;
you forgive me generously and stay at my side.
It was your pleasure to bring us together.
Bless the Lord, O my soul:
Let all that is within me bless God's holy name. Amen

Ian M. Fraser

I love them

Dear God
Thank you for my mum and dad
I love them
Thank you for my brother
Thank you for my pets.

Prayers from Hackwood Park School

Prayer at my son's 21st

Dear God, today my son is twenty-one.
My child has grown.
My baby gone, replaced by this ...
When did it happen?
Did I miss the growing?
Can I really believe I have a son who's taller than me,
and who tells me so – with pride?

Dear God,
today I see no child of mine
but this grown man who's part of me.
I ask no prayers for him –
for he will pray (or not, as he will choose)
for his own needs,
better known to him than me.
So, on this day I pray for myself,
that I may worthy stand
with this young man,
and be the father now he needs me to be.

Tom Gordon

Blessing for child and carer

Lord, a threefold blessing I ask for this child in my care:

safety and courage to walk as a lamb among wolves,
health to grow as strong as a shoot that will bear good fruit,
and delight of freedom to fly like wild geese on the Spirit's wind.

A threefold blessing I ask for myself in my caring:

love to forgive always,
wisdom to learn as much as I teach,
and open arms, both to welcome and to let go.

Annie Heppenstall-West

My family

God,
can you stop my family arguing?

Prayers from Hackwood Park School

A blessing for Shiisa

May the love of God encompass and protect you.
May the wisdom of God teach and nurture you.
May the fire of God kindle you
to be a flame of love to your neighbour
all your days. Amen

Jean E.S. Williams

The presence of your saints and angels

Loving God, I ask for your surrounding,
for the presence of your saints and angels
with my loved ones this night.

May your light temper their darkness.
May your grace gladden their dreams.
May your strong love uphold their spirits.
May your deep care soothe their weary hearts.

And in the morning when we meet,
may the joy of the knowledge of your presence
pass between us and among us as a sweet kiss of peace. Amen

Yvonne Morland

Ourselves

Our loveliness

Loving Christ,
in love you were made and made us.
Help us to accept our loveliness,
and, as we reach out to our neighbour,
help us to know that we, too, are precious.[4]

Kate McIlhagga

Thank you

Thank you for making my life
and everyone else's special.
Thank you for my toys and computer.

Prayers from Hackwood School

In good days and bad days

God
You tell me
I am as important as my neighbour

I am precious
in your sight

You know and recognise
my name

My life has meaning
and purpose

I am loved
and liked
and cherished

I belong
in your world.

God
in my good days and bad days
help me
to hear you affirm
your delight in me.

Beckon me into your joy.

Ruth Burgess

Grow up

I thought that if I abased myself before you, Lord God,
you would approve. It is a biblical thing to do.
The psalmist cried, 'I am a worm and no man.'*
And Isaiah: 'Can the pot question the potter's know-how?'+
So I scraped around searching for things to confess
that would make me small and worthless and guilty before you.
But you said, 'Cut out the crap.
Stand on your feet; hold your head high.
You are no worm. You are no clay pot.
You are my friend, made in my likeness.
Grow up! Look like who you are.'
You put me right. Good for you, Lord. Thanks. Amen

Ian M. Fraser

*Psalm 22:6; +Isaiah 45:9

We have love

God our maker, our mother, our father,
you have gifted us
and nurtured us
and journeyed with us.
We are who we are because of you.

We are people with hearts full of love,
bodies ready to work,
minds ready to explore.

You ask us to follow you and work with you but we are hesitant.
We have not always been encouraged to believe in ourselves,
we dwell on our failures,
we are over-modest.

In silence
we search our hearts and minds
to discover what we might never have thought of giving to you.
We name what we have within us to offer to you and our world ...
We have love.
We have skills.
We have potential.

Take us, God.
Take our love and skills and potential.
Give us confidence to be the people you want us to be.

(This prayer may be followed by the chant 'Take, O take me as I am'.)

Alison Adam

You take me seriously

I settle into stillness
searching
seeking
trusting your joy

My mind races
and you embrace it
wrapping me round
with wonder and grace

You wrestle with me
question me
take me seriously
I bless the honesty of your love.

Ruth Burgess

Justice and peace

Why God?

Oh God,
why is everyone having wars?
We're in the middle of it just now.
Can't you make peace with everyone?
Why can't everyone be friends?

Prayers from Hackwood Park School

Believe in one another

God our challenger and disturber,
help us to confront
all that makes for death and despair
in our lives, our communities, our world.
May we never lose sight
of the possibility of transformation
and be continually surprised
by people who believe in one another.

Joy Mead

Outrageous for the Kingdom's sake

I'm in a quandary, Lord.
I take a plane and add to pollution,
yet inter-relationships across the world enrich and enlarge life.
I buy goods from poor countries

and may unwittingly encourage exploitation of labour.
So teach me your way of righteousness, Holy God:
that I devote time and intellect to digging out hidden factors,
followed by letters to MPs, protest marches, withdrawal of taxes.
Make me outrageous for the Kingdom's sake,
even if I should get clobbered as was Jesus Christ.
I ask strength for this in his name. Amen

Ian M. Fraser

Love of difference

God of longings,
give us
sensitivity to the needs of others
and a deep love of difference;
the desire to be connected with people;
the deep wish that others may grow
and follow their dreams;

and the wisdom to know
that this is peace.

Joy Mead

Peace without justice

Peace without justice
doesn't work,
does it God?

It doesn't work for nations.
It doesn't work for individuals.

Question my activities,
challenge my priorities,
lay bare my careless opinions,
root your integrity in my life.

Ruth Burgess

The greatest gift

Thank you for your greatest of gifts:
a sense of humour.
For with it we
celebrate life
express joy
laugh and feel release
enjoy the absurd
puncture pride
explode self-importance

put things in perspective
share a joke
discover common ground.

For peace starts with a smile.

Zam Walker Coleman

Peace be with you and also with your spirit
A prayer meditation

Images of peace:
a dove
white lilies
a calm sea
candles.

Yet what does our inner peace
feel and look like?

May the peace of the Lord be always with you.

Rosie Morton

Hearts may begin to change

Father,
we look at the world and its pain.
Touch our hearts and hear our prayers,
both for those in need
and for those causing the misery,
that, by your power,
hearts may begin to change. Amen

Jean Murdoch

God's dream of Shalom

God, your dream is challenging.
It is tough and direct.
You expect much of us,
and we have much to give.

Only you
can prepare us for your way.

So, where we are hard-hearted, disturb our indifference,
where we feel far from you, come close to us,
where we feel useless, reveal your hidden potential,
where we feel dejected, hold us in your love.

We commit ourselves to the journey inward.
We open our hearts to you
so that, nourished and sustained,
we may be more fruitful on the journey outward.

We are willing to be your hands,
ready to be your feet,
eager to open our eyes to look out in compassion on the world.

Mark us as your own
as we make our mark –
a sign of our yes to you.

(This prayer may be followed by the singing of a chant, e.g. 'In love you summon, in love I follow', during which people are invited to make a mark – a sign of their commitment to God. This may be marking an 'X' on a 'ballot paper', signing their name, anointing themselves on the palm with oil ...)

Alison Adam

With those who ...

With those who would kill themselves to kill others
We pray for peace

With those who want to build up nuclear weapons
We pray for peace

With those who want to inflict terror and fear
We pray for peace

With those who want war
We pray for peace.

Rosie Miles

Peace

Three-in-One,
an eternal knot,
bind us to you.

Three-in-One,
unravel knots
of fear and hate.

Three-in-One,
entangle us
with peace.

Mary Taylor

Jesus, stiller of storms

Jesus, stiller of storms,
still the storms in our hearts and minds,
the rage of anger, the turbulence of fear,
and bring us your peace.

Kathy Galloway

Regrets, hopes and graces

Denying the Spirit

Oh God, we are doing it all the time. Why?
Where there is something truly good,
why are we denying it?
When someone has courage to be different,
why are we decrying it?
Why do we rubbish what is most precious –
the pearl of your presence
why do we trample it underfoot?
Why, when we see a flickering flame,
do we try to blow it out?
Why do we believe that only we are right?

Stop us in our tracks, God,
dazzle us with different ways
your Spirit is at work in the world.
Teach us to be humble, to be open to receive.
Help us to recognise your presence
in other folk – and to be moved
beyond respect, to reverence. Amen

Jan Sutch Pickard

Prayer of approach

God,
You are no lucky charm,
no rabbit's foot,
no plastic Jesus.

You take mess and make meaning,
you take confusion and offer faith,
you take repentance and offer healing,
you take darkness and balance it with light,
so that,
in slog and sleep,
your goodness might be tasted and enjoyed.

Amazing and surprising God,
you are no mere excuse for our gathering
for you promise to be part of it,
not to force your word upon us
but to speak to those who want to listen,
perhaps to nudge those who need to listen,
and to warn those whose minds are closed.

David Coleman

Getting help

Dear God
I wish I was not naughty
I wish I could get some help to get to sleep
I like to get help to do things.

Prayers from Hackwood Park School

Grace and generosity

God, you love with such grace and generosity.
Forgive me for the ways I reject others and myself.

God, you reveal true beauty.
Forgive me for judging by appearances.

God, you promise to keep me safe.
Forgive me for clinging to an earthly security because I can.

God, you tell me that you will catch me if I fall.
Forgive me for my lack of trust in you and in your people.

God, you wait to heal and renew.
Forgive me for hurting others because I am hurting.

Loving God,
help me to respond to your love,
your beauty, your safety, your healing.

Deb Buckley

A regrettable prayer

Good God,
what a mess!

Father,
come and collect your lost child.

Jesus,
come and deal with your disciple who gets things wrong.

Holy Spirit,
come and refill this body, your temple.

Over to you, God,
I'm in your hands now.
What will you make of me?

Back to square one at my time of life?
O Christ!

Ian Cowie

Grace is never wasted

Forgiving God,
we remember in your presence
the graceful moments we have wasted –
the times we have turned our backs
on sunrise and sunset;
our failure to meet the eyes of others
or to open our hearts;
the shared silences we have filled up with words ...
Turn us round, God.
Bring us face to face.
Help us to trust each other.
Speak your healing word –
and may our silence sing. Amen

Jan Sutch Pickard

To live hopefully

God help us to live fully and openly and hopefully,
to trust in grace
and believe in resurrection.

Neil Paynter

Open hands

God of open hands and once upon a time moments,
help us to extend the boundaries of the possible
and continually re-dream the world.

Joy Mead

You seek us out

God of grace,
you seek us out
when we hide from you,
you call our name
when we least expect to hear,
you believe in us
when we live in doubt.
Lay hold of our hearts,
our minds, our lives,
as we commit ourselves afresh
to loving one another,
accepting ourselves
and proclaiming your justice in the world.

Elizabeth Baxter

Like trees beside a river

God of transformation, refresh us with living water,
take us out of our depth, trusting in you;
nourish the roots we often forget –
our deepest feelings and our dreams –
so that we may grow like trees beside a river,
standing tall, and bearing fruit. Amen

Jan Sutch Pickard

Hurt and healing

Why?

Why do you let people die if you love us?
Why do you let people hurt and cry inside?
Why do you let people get cuts and bruises?
Why do you let people have nasty accidents?

Prayers from Hackwood Park School

The campsite

I will boast about my weakness
so that Christ's power may come to rest upon me. *

If weakness
is the sort of campsite you like, Lord,
there's a great one here for you,
with plenty of space.

Pitch your tent on my weakness.
My stronghold was never up to much anyway.

Ian Cowie

*2 Corinthians 12:9

Christ, my cornerstone

I feel depression
enter my being like
cold rain
seeping
into a poorly constructed building.

O God of the fragile and broken,
set me with a firm foundation,
make Christ my cornerstone,
heal me.

Neil Paynter

Hold me there

God who touched the untouchables,
reach out to me in my darkness.
Bring me once again
into the glorious light of your love
and hold me there.

Joyce Clarke

Handle me gently

Handle me gently, if you please –

for life is fragile,
a heart so easily broken,
a spirit so easily crushed.
Lean on me, and I will crumble
returning to the dust whence I came.
Blow on me, and a myriad pieces
will float away like the seeds
of a dandelion clock,
never to return.
Push me, and the shattered remnants
of the jigsaw
will never complete the picture.
Love me, and there may yet be hope.
Hold me in your prayers
and place me within the circle of God's love.

Handle me gently, if you please.

Cath Threlfall

I found a lump

I found a lump. I'm scared.
Cancer.
Not death, but too much life.

Cells out of balance
like sin; life at others' expense.

It's a shock. I feel so healthy.

God our refuge,
help me to adjust, to take on board my new reality.
Enable me to cope with what lies ahead:
the bewildering options and difficult decisions,
the surgery and further treatment.
Save me in this time of trial.

But I remember
You did not say, 'You will not be tested.'
You said, 'You shall not be overcome.'

God, light in our darkness,
strengthen me to face each day and to live it well.

Zam Walker Coleman

Help me to let go

Help me to trust you God
help me to trust my friends
help me to put down the hurt of my living
help me to let go.

Ruth Burgess

Prayer for a service of healing

I pray for the Holy Spirit
to come to you
and tend your wounds.

I pray for you,
beloved child of God,
beautiful but hurt,
strong but sometimes scared.

I pray that you may grow
in gentleness of spirit
and learn to trust people again,
to give and to receive.

I pray that you find the openings
in the walls of fear and pain
and move,
step by step,
towards a new beginning
of sharing and freedom,
of laughter and love.

May She come to you
with a lover's tenderness
and heal you,
body, mind and spirit,
of all that harms you.
Amen

Gerke van Hiele

Until the light comes again

O my God,
when the dark clouds gather –
when my spirits are low,
when my body mocks me,
when my heart is closed to the love of your people,
when my eyes are closed to the beauty of your creation –
then, Lord, let me feel your arms around me
until the light comes again.

Andrew Foster

Greet the dawn

God of shadows and echoes, darkness and light,
help us to be still in our dark moments,
our waiting times, our uncertainties.
And when morning comes,
show us how to greet the dawn
without trying to make sense
of the amazing light.

Joy Mead

A reminder

People
places
institutions
situations
can put me down.

God
only
ever
wants
to raise me up
and love me.

Alleluia
Amen

Ruth Burgess

The Spirit of new life

Here in the heart of God,
here in the heart of love
welcoming all our weakness –
the Spirit of new life.

da *Noust*

Credo

The ache in my side

You are the ache in my side,
all the hunger.

You are my longing
and the hard struggle
to become whole.

You are the face of my desire.

Rosie Miles

As I breathe

God our father and our mother
    as I breathe so I pray

Amen

Rosie Morton

My centre

You are my centre
deep within;
the place I return to
when tempted by sin.

You are my apex
high above;
the point that I aim for
when prompted by love.

I walk in your footsteps,
you walk in mine;
knowing companions
in communion through time. Amen

Yvonne Morland

Statement of faith

God does not leave me.
I do not leave God.
God is.
I am.

Annie Heppenstall-West

I stand

In your holy presence
I stand.

In the glory of your creation
I stand.

In the midst of saints and angels
I stand.

Catch me quickly God
for my knees
are trembling.

Ruth Burgess

Mysterious but true

When I was younger I knew
which way was up.
Faith meant learning the facts
from parents, priests, pedagogues –
people who already knew them.
Things like The Trinity and pi were mysterious, but
true all the same.

Now that I'm old enough to be wiser,
facts ain't what they used to be.

God is still mysterious,
that hasn't changed –
if, that is, God is.
I have learnt one thing though:
not to expect certainties,
just to muddle along from moment to moment
in the dark
redefining faith,
searching for hope,
needing love.

Frances Copsey

I have come thus far

So I have come thus far, Lord God.
As I look over my life, I wonder what you make of it.
I know that human measures of success or failure don't apply –
on the cross, Jesus was a failure to human eyes.
But you know better, and it is to you I have to give account of my life.
I realise I'll get a shock when I see my life through your eyes.
But I also know the love of Jesus Christ for ordinary people
doing ordinary things to keep life going,
and his special compassion for those who have it rough and tough.
When my time comes I'll not rest my case.
I'll just rest my bones, trusting in him. Amen

Ian M. Fraser

Desert believing

Grant me faith
to hold to what once I knew,
that you are there beside me,
loving, caring, healing,
gently guiding
the course of my journey.

Grant me faith
in the dry dust about me,
in the bleak emptiness
that waits,
that yearns,
that longs for you again.

Grant me faith to believe
that in this aching void
somewhere there is another milestone,
another knowing,
or unknowing,
of your infinite mystery.

Chris Polhill

Daily living

God of ordinary life

God of ordinary life, be in my life.
God of deepest joy, be in my joys.
God of agonising pain, share my pain.
God of wisdom, work on me.
God of humility, walk with me.

Joyce Clarke

A blessing for daily work

Christ the worker,
builder of solid foundations,
teller of tales about baking and business and cleaning,
brother of ordinary folk,

your blessing on my work I ask,
your yoke for my shoulders I pray –
your sense of purpose,
your willingness to serve.

Annie Heppenstall-West

Mothers' prayer/checklist

Please God …

1. Can I have more time?
2. Help me to make it before the school bell
3. Make my lipstick straight
4. My skirt neat – not tucked into my knickers
5. Let the childminder be in
6. Let my diary and purse be in my bag
7. Let the clock be fast
8. Let me appear to be organised, with no stains on my clothes, no labels showing
9. Give me a happy smile
   to do your work with grace and style

Thanks God. Did I say Amen? Amen

Louise Glen-Lee

Suppose

I suppose I ought to thank You
for the knocking door
crying cot
flashing answer-phone
bomb-hit-it desk
crashed computer
and everything else,
just as you are getting down to it.

I suppose …
But bugger that!
Why stretch the list?
Thanks instead
for space enough to scream.

Let it be so!
Amen

David Coleman

Life is a gift

Life is a gift
but
(and there's always a but)
sometimes it feels like
falling into a combine harvester
and then
I want to give it back.

Frances Copsey

Prayer at the start of a difficult meeting

Living God, as we address the business before us, grant us wisdom and insight, sensitivity and tolerance. Help us to listen carefully to one another's views, and to think before we speak. And, when we come to decide the way ahead, may we be blessed with courage and imagination and the hope that comes from you. Amen

Norman Shanks

Sunshine

Dear God
It is a gloomy day
I hope we can have some sunshine today
I need it.

Benjamin (aged 8)

Prayer for teachers

Remind us, Lord,
that we have no idea
what is really going on
behind the closed doors
of some pupils'
eyes, hearts, minds,
relationships and home lives.
Keep us caring
in spite of
the 'no entry' signs.

Pam Hathorn

Prayer for guidance

Gracious God, I am struggling to discern your will: I cannot make my mind up; my thoughts are confused, and the advice of my friends is not clear. In and through the darkness, help me with a strong sense of your loving kindness. Give me patience not to rush my decision. Help me to set aside all the petty concerns that sully my mind and heart. Open up my life with a readiness to be surprised by the joy and freedom of the way of Jesus Christ. Amen

Norman Shanks

Living with cancer

Thank you for giving me a wake-up call:
to look at the world with new eyes,
to live NOW –
not stuck in the past,
not fretting life away for an unknown and unknowable future.
Thank you for giving me the chance to look at my life afresh.

I know to trust you and not worry:
to live fully and value each unique and precious moment,
to cherish each part of your creation,
to seek you in each person I meet,
to live with joy,
which I have too often denied.

Thank you for blessing me.

Zam Walker Coleman

A prayer of reflection after the departure of visitors

Phew!
At last they're gone
safely away,
I guess they did enjoy their stay.

Anon.

A thank you prayer

For games to play and friends to share,
for fun in the water and sand,
for warm and sunny days,
thank you God.

Prayers from Hackwood Park School

The last enslaving power

Lord God, you know me.
You know how I preened myself yesterday ...
Sexual excess can take over my life? Drugs, drink, tobacco?
I was in the clear!
That was till the last enslaving power was noted – shopping.

With cupboards crammed and wardrobes bulging, I confess my inability
    to rein in my desires.
I confess money spent on myself that should have gone to those in want.
I confess failure to investigate production practices that might exploit
    and enslave others who make goods I covet.

I, who make out I am in charge of my own life, am, myself, a slave.

Lord Christ, who rids the possessed of demons,
save me and help me,
I humbly beseech you, O Lord. Amen

Ian M. Fraser

God of all calm

God of all calm,

In the midst of this turmoil
give me hope
that again I will live
a day
with little anxiety,
like the day
we spent by the sea
when the waves
washed in
washed out
washed in again
and cleansed
this troubled mind.

God of all calm,
give me hope.

Louise Glen-Lee

A prayer for Peggy

God remembers you:
your name and your story,
today
and every day;

in the darkness before morning
you are not alone;

in the questions without answers
you are not unheard.

Whatever happens to you,
you will always be yourself.

God is on your road;
God walks with you
all the smiles
and tears of your journey.

Today and every day,
God remembers you
with love.

Ruth Burgess

In your work

In your work
may you know joy
and a sense of achievement.

May you use your talents
and feel fulfilled.

May you have moments of fun,
of friendship and laughter.

When the going is tough,
may you bring good
out of adverse situations.

May you have courage
to speak out against injustice.

May you refrain from gossip.

May you have the wisdom to know
when it is time to move on
and let go. Amen

Mary Taylor

Prayer for inspiration and creativity

God of light and love, I am so frustrated that, faced with this deadline, wanting to respond to this opportunity, I am bereft of worthwhile ideas and my imagination has run dry.

By the miracle of your grace, find a spark of energy to fire my dull mind and my dead heart with the vision of your kingdom, that the words and thoughts may flow once more to your glory. Amen

Norman Shanks

Into your love

Loving God,
at this moment there are many people who think
that no one is praying for them.
Please lift them into your love
and hold them there.
They need to be sure they are not forgotten.

Joyce Clarke

Prayer of praise

Warm as the summer sunshine,
We praise you for your love, O Lord.
Plentiful as the rain on the hills,
We praise you for your love, O Lord.
Caring as a mother holding her child,
We praise you for your love, O Lord.
Gentle as the waves lapping the seashore,
We praise you for your love, O Lord.
Powerful as the wind that bends the trees,
We praise you for your love, O Lord.
Pure as the whiteness of fresh winter snow,
We praise you for your love, O Lord.
Forgiving as the friend who bears no grudge,
We praise you for your love, O Lord.
Continuous as the circle that has no ending,
We praise you for your love, O Lord.

Simon Taylor

Grace after attending the Edinburgh Festival

Creator Spirit, our ears are filled with the beauty of sound,
our eyes are gladdened by the richness of colour and form,
our imaginations are tumbling with new ideas.
For all of these things, we thank you.

Jean E.S. Williams

Our world

Thank you for food, water and clothes,
thank you for families, friends and homes,
thank you for trees, grass and flowers,
thank you for laughter, happiness and rest.
God, thank you for our world.

Prayers from Hackwood Park School

I am grateful for my day

Thank you God
that today I have eaten well, basked in the sunshine,
read a good book, enjoyed the company of friends.
Life is good.

As I rejoice,
help me to not forget those who have found this day drear –
without food, without comfort –
and who will find the same tomorrow.

I am grateful for my day, God.
Help me to turn my gratitude
away from words and into action,
for your sake. Amen

Joyce Clarke

Moments of our days

Birth

We pray for those awaiting a birth:
the birth of a child, the birth of an idea,
the birth of new hope out of despair.
We pray for those who give birth in difficult conditions,
for those who long for a child but cannot have one,
for those facing unwanted pregnancy.
Lead us in ways of love for them,
for the sake of Mary and the child Jesus.

Kathy Galloway

Deep as the earth, free as the wind

May our love be as wild as fire
as free as the wind
as deep as the earth
as gentle as a running stream.

May our love bring to birth a child.

Mary Taylor

Growing

Dear God
I wish I was older
and could do what I want.

Prayers from Hackwood Park School

A sequence of Marker Stone blessings

Birth

For this new little one
God's blessings abound.

Healthy growing,
learning, knowing;
life's gentle wonder,
potential showing.

Friends to play with,
laughing, crying;
life's harsher blunders
loving arms surround.

Holy Spirit flow round
this new little one.

Menarche

That first blood flowing
so life may be
a child may be
born
one day.

God bless this body
woman now
bleeding now

shape
changing.

Encircle her with love.

Leaving home

Excitement and fear I lay before you,
for your blessing,
for your grace.

On the freedom and the chances,
on the growing,
the new place,
set your blessing and your grace.

They've gone

Tidy lounge, unrumpled beds;
no seven-hole boots or hairy legs.
No deep male laughter.
Just quiet.

And the grieving.
Cord-wrenched, womb-torn, weeping sadness.

And rejoicing.
Grown them, free and strong, from babe to man.

Bless their nest-flown flying
on the winds of life's storm.
Bless this new beginning,
this creative, empty space.

Menopause

The rhythm of life,
that pulse for new life,
pattern of each lunar month,

preparing the place –
a chance to create
endless possibilities.

Written now in my soul
as it was in my body;
God's rhythm within me
not ending, just changing.

Anniversary

Celebrate and bless them,
married long, loving more.

Celebrate and bless them,
twisting tough and joyful –
one flesh, freedom's space,
in God's dance discern their steps.

Celebrate and bless them,
these two in one who live your love.

Meeting mystery

Those timeless moments
of searing beauty
bless me still:

Eternal sea dance of wave and sun,
dawn's bright beams under cloudy skies,
birdsong, a child's face,
a candle burning.

Yet all pale to dust beside that moment
when God's beauty
caught my heart
to stillness.
She blesses me still.
God blesses me still.

Divorce

Take this failure,
broken vows.
Take the pain,
mistakes, lost hopes.

Not forgetting there was fun,
not forgetting there was good.

Take them; mulch them;
mix them; turn them
to be your rich compost
for the new ground we tread.

God bless this new beginning.
God bless us, life renewing.

50

Gawd bless me,
I'm blinking fifty!
More than 'alf me time'as gawn!

So thanks fer all so far.
Even takin' rough wiv smoov,
life's just a gift, so ta.

An' 'scuse me fer askin',
but keep me livin', not existin',
till me time is due.

An' now I'm fifty, reely fifty!
P'raps I'll take a risk or two
fer You.

Chris Polhill

Ageing

Dear God, someone I love is ageing,
becoming a person I don't know,
reminding me that I am ageing too.

Help us both to travel well
in this new relationship with life,
with the world, with each other and with you.

Let each moment in the present
hold something of your grace,
free of any troubles from the past.

Guide us through our fears and frailties,
good companions on the way,
till each can rest at home with you, at last.

Yvonne Morland

Remember me in my dying

Lord of all life,
when others died I thought of death as part of nature:
a rose flourishing, bestowing fragrance, and returning to the earth.
Now that death draws nearer me
it is not fear, but wonder that fills me,
when I think of the speck of life I was in the womb
and what I tried to accomplish over the years.

For death itself I trust Jesus's promises;
but dying may be hard to bear,
possibly in unremitting pain with the body out of control,
a stranger to the mind.
Lord of all life, remember me in my dying:
remember us all in our dying. Amen

Ian M. Fraser

Dancing in the streets

When my time comes
please, please, please
no penguin parades,
no solemn posturing:
but folk in jeans,
children playing, babies crying
and dancing in the streets.

Ian M. Fraser

Morning and evening

As the sun rises

As the sun rises,
bringing light into dark places,
enabling life to flourish on the earth,
so, Lord, come into our dark places
with your light and hope
and renew us with your life.

Margaret Harvey

Grace for a new day

God of the sunrise,
who gives us this day
in all its beauty
all its opportunities
all its challenges
all its new relationships,
we give you thanks.
Guide our paths,
suggest our actions,
be in us
and in those we meet,
through Jesus Christ, our Lord.
Amen

Jean E.S. Williams

God of the morning

God of the morning,
help us to be still:
to breathe
to be aware
to appreciate
the giftedness of today
the sounds
the colours
the tastes
the tasks and people waiting.
Help us to explore the mystery
opening before us
all around us
and deep within us.

Lead us into the life of this new day.

Lynda Wright

The adventure of this new day

Lord of life, we praise you for all that is:
for the reaches of our star-studded space,
for the particles small beyond imagining,
for the detailed immensity of your love,
for the promise of your companionship
through the adventure of this new day.

Margaret Harvey

Prayer and blessing to counter the Monday morning feeling

This is the day the Lord has made
and, by Christ,
I am going to live it!
Live it with every fibre of my being!
I will enter wholeheartedly
into every experience, pleasant or unpleasant.
I'm going to give it everything I've got.

Another week ...
Here we go, Lord.

Be strong and of good courage.
Be not afraid or dismayed
for the Lord your God is with you
wherever you may go.

Ian Cowie

Gentle God of evening time

Gentle God of this
evening time,
we pause now,
listening into the stillness
for an awareness of
your presence.
Breathing out,
letting go –
our tiredness,
our frustrations,
our anxieties.
Giving ourselves to you,
that you may hold
us in your peace.

Lynda Wright

Turn us with the earth

Car parked
supper savoured
bath wallowed
a good book and
sleep to come.

Thank you for another day.

Bless those I met today:
those I worry about
those who are strong and well
those who need help
those I watched on the news
those I talked with on the phone
those I find demanding
those who find me annoying
those I love.

Watch over them
watch over me
guard us sleeping
greet us waking
turn us, with the earth,
into light and life.

Ruth Burgess

The day is ending

Lord, the day is ending and our work is almost done.
May the clamour of voices,
the insistence of telephones,
the clattering and glare of our computers,
all be stilled as we turn towards you.
We pray that your blessings of peace and rest
may be ours throughout the night,
refreshing us for tomorrow and for all the new days to come.

Andrew Foster

The seasons turning

Awakening

Praise be to God
for winter awakening to spring,
for budding branches bare against a sunlit sky
and the tough fragility of snowdrops
speaking of promise to come.
Praise be to God
for the stirring of hope
and new dreams growing.

Jan Berry

Warm God of summer

Warm God of summer,
strewer of petals,
ripener of fruits

delight in us,
revel in us,
mellow us in joy.

Ruth Burgess

Rich for me

Straight, golden grasses
tipped with copper
vibrant green at base
gently swaying in the breeze.

Sunshine catching
precious jewels in autumn,
rich for me.

Jenny Ayre

Mid-November afternoon

I rake the sodden leaves; scrape the knotted, root-filled earth;
vainly sniff the last rosebud that cannot open
as the damp seeps through and browns each petal's golden hue.
It's very still.
A blackbird lights upon the compost heap.
A sparrow in the privet hedge makes bright announcement to his mate.
A strange resonance now in the grey, moisture-holding air:
In damp-dying and putrefying death, Creator God,
You are here.

Liz Gregory-Smith

A communion prayer

Walking home in the cloudy cold night and suddenly
the smell of snow
like bread rising;

and I shut my eyes
and hold out my tongue to catch
the first slow, dizzy flakes
dancing in the lamplight.

Make me a clean heart, O God.
Set a new and right spirit within me.

Make me a joyful child.
Make me a joyful child.

Neil Paynter

All the presents

God
thank you for birthdays, Christmas, New Year, Easter,
and all the presents.

Prayers from Hackwood Park School

A new year's beginning

Hold us God
we need you

wrap us up in the shawl
of your loving,
cradle us in your arms

walk with us
into a new dawn
a new year's beginning

dance with us into
the delights and dangers
of your turning world.

Ruth Burgess

The renewing of the earth

Creator God, whose faithfulness is seen
in the coming and going of the seasons,
whose love is seen in the renewing of the earth;
guard and guide us,
keep and bless us,
now and for evermore. Amen

Simon Taylor

Advent and Christmas

An Advent prayer

As the year
turns again
into darkness,
cradle us
bright holy God.

Warm us
with wonder.

Safeguard us
with courage.

Trust us
with justice.

Quicken us
with love.

Ruth Burgess

Another Advent prayer

Wet days
Long nights
Red candles
Old songs

Warm us God
Wrap us round with wonder

Furl us deep
into your joy and justice
Love us
through the moments
of our nights and days.

Ruth Burgess

What can I give you?

I saw Santa on Saturday, Lord.
Your birthday is coming on Christmas morning,
what can I give you?

Prayers from Hackwood Park School

The story of love and life

Storytelling God,
sit us down by the fire of your strong love
this Christmas.
Warm us with your glory.
Welcome us to the feast.
Tell us again
amidst the tears and laughter,
the story of the cross and the cradle,
the story of love and life.

Ruth Burgess

Help us to light a candle

O God, we watch the news
and we read the headlines
about crime, cruelty and abuse.
We don't want people to be hurt –
but what can we do to help?
Light of the world,
where there is darkness
Help us to light a candle.

O God, we look around us
and we see that people are lonely
and unhappy. Some are unfaithful.
They say they don't care for anyone.
We care – but what can we do?
Light of the world,
where there is darkness
Help us to light a candle.

O God, we live in the world.
We know there is hunger and poverty,
and that so many things are unfair.
We can raise money, we can raise our voices,
we can change the way we live.
Light of the world,
where there is darkness
Help us to light a candle.

O God, you came into the world
in the baby Jesus, at Christmas.
Your love is the good news
that the angels told to ordinary people.
Take us, ordinary people,
and help us to put our faith into action.
Light of the world,
where there is darkness
Help us to light a candle.

Prayers from Tobermory High School

Christmas Eve

Emmanuel, God with us,
heaven come down to earth,
help us tonight to listen to the angels
and not to be afraid of you,
of your weakness or your glory.
Come, holy helpless Jesus,
come into our lives with joy.

Ruth Burgess

Three prayers for a Christmas Eucharist

Gathering

Emmanuel,
born of stardust
and earth's squalor,
embrace
our foolishness
into your wisdom,
our coldness
into your warmth:
that together
we may heal
all that wounds,
and open the door
to friendship.

Prayer after Communion

Home-gatherer
we have found ourselves
welcomed,
cherished and fed;
our stable
lit by stars;

our fears
stroked by angels' wings.

Take us with you
as you beckon others,
drawing the world
to your hearth,
and the hungry
to your table

Blessing

Christmas child,
curl your fingers round ours in blessing.
Your clasp
secures us;
your trust
challenges us;
and your presence
unites us,
this holy season
and for all time.
Amen

Elizabeth Baxter

Saviour of all pilgrim people

Only God would christen Jesus
with a name that faith reveals as
saviour of all pilgrim people –
those who trek by silver light.

Heartbeat close, his parents cradle
Jesus, born within a stable;
see the cult of power disabled –
God is born for humankind.

Stars appear and promise daybreak;
violent soldiers herald heartache;
cries of anguish pierce the darkness –
where is God in human need?

Word made flesh, our gifts revealing;
Mary, Joseph, persevering;
all who find God's gift amazing
turn for home by unknown ways.

da *Noust*

Lent, Easter
and Pentecost

Barefooted

Loving and compassionate God,
lead us this Lent
on to ground which is holy.
Beckon us barefooted
and without luggage
into your justice and joy.

Ruth Burgess

Collects for Lent

Ash Wednesday (Is. 58:1–12)

O God, advocate of all who are oppressed,
You shatter our illusions of righteousness
and unmask our divided hearts,
in order that we might be filled with longing for justice and generosity
and so be made whole.
As justice for those who work
and generosity for those who cannot,
are true marks of a heart turning towards you,
let our actions as well as our intentions
bear witness to the longing of our hearts.

First Sunday in Lent (Matt. 4:1–11)

O Christ, who entered into the lonely desert,
and who, facing hunger, danger and temptation

did not turn aside
but affirmed the way of self-giving love;
strengthen us to resist the false attraction of easy answers,
magic fixes,
abuses of power,
and the delusion that there is any way apart from justice
in which God's justice can be done.

Second Sunday in Lent (John 3:1–17)

O Christ, as you were lifted up upon the cross,
exposed for all the world to see, and sneer, and abandon;
give us courage not to abandon those also exposed
by poverty, unemployment or stigma
to the risk of unprotected living,
and faith to believe that even we
may be born again
in the Spirit of love.

Third Sunday in Lent (John 4:5–42)

O Christ, as you spoke with the woman at the well
and drank from her cup
to the scandal of your disciples,
because of her indignity;
grant that we who are habitually scandalised
by everyone except ourselves
may learn from you to refrain from judgement,
to accord respect to all God's children,
and so be privileged to hear the witness
of those the world treats with indignity.

Fourth Sunday in Lent (John 9:1–41)

O Christ our enlightener,
once and for all,
you broke the link between suffering and punishment,
erased the line between deserving and undeserving
and invited the unseeing to open their eyes to the truth about themselves.
Doing this, you revealed yourself,
became vulnerable.
Preserve us from the defendedness that makes us vicious,
give us insight to see the structures of injustice by which we profit,
and grace to cherish all people in our vulnerability,
knowing that we all live within your love.

Fifth Sunday in Lent (John 11:1–45)

O Christ, lover and friend,
who felt the desolation of death
and the fear of abandonment
and yet practised *'yes'* in the midst of each despairing *'no'*;
may we, who also recognise the shape of desolation
and weep,
practise *'no'* in the midst of each complicit *'yes'*.
No to profiteering and exploitation,
no to indifference and abuse,
no for the sake of the resurrection *yes*.

Holy Week

O Christ, you entered the city as a poor man,
not in style but simply,

yet still you caused uproar, and questions everywhere;
you drew the expectations of a hungry crowd,
and brought buried conflicts to the light.
May we, who are sometimes swayed by the crowd's approval,
and who often avoid conflict
for fear of its cost to us,
hold fast to the gospel of truth and justice
and follow faithfully in your way of compassion and solidarity
with those who are poor and excluded,
wherever it may lead us.

Easter

O Christ, today, gloriously, joyfully, you live for ever
in the life of the world,
in the hearts of those who love you,
in the power of the Spirit to transcend even death.
May we who love you, and find in you our hope,
bear witness, as Thomas did,
that your risen body still carries the marks
of the world's violence, injustice and greed,
and as we remember and rejoice,
help us to keep faith with all who still, today,
suffer the outrages of violence, injustice and greed.
In our actions, in our prayers, in our choices and in our commitment,
teach us the true meaning of good news for the poor.

Kathy Galloway

Easter Monday

Giving God,
forgive us for the times
when we are too busy
to see the beauty of your creation all around us;
too fearful
to hear the Good News of the empty tomb;
too set in our ways
to set out on your way.   Amen

Jan Sutch Pickard

A prayer for Pentecost

Bright God of life:
burn in our lives
blow us clean and holy
bless us with courage and joy
refine in us your justice
blaze in us all our days.

Ruth Burgess

Goodness, joy and loving kindness

Come, Holy Spirit:

As the green flames of spring
sweep through the woods
promising plenty,

come sweep through our lives
and bring to fruit in us
your goodness,
your joy
and your loving kindness.

John Ayre

Prayers for the journey

God of our journeying

God of all our journeying,
inviting us to travel with you,
forgive us when we cling to outworn security,
afraid to let go of what is safe and familiar.

Give us courage
to take the risk
of answering your call
into joyous adventure.

Jan Berry

Surprise

Surprise us, Lord,

for surprises keep us hopeful.

They stir behind the musty folds of our weariness
then rush out,
shouting in glorious unpredictability.

They spin us round till our eyes are full of dizzying stars –
a galaxy of miracles.

Go on ... surprise us, Lord.

Jim Hughes

Such a God

Lord God,
what can we make of such a God as we find you to be?
'Surprise me!' you keep on saying. 'Surprise me.'
We offer you unquestioning obedience, dogged faithfulness,
blameless characters no one can fault.
You respond, 'Surprise me!'
'Do you mean us to walk on water?' we ask.
You say, 'That's been done. Dance on water.'

What can we make of such a God?
How like you to ask of us impossible things
and to set our feet tapping.

Ian M. Fraser

Pull me towards heaven

Angels
shelter me
in the shadow
of your presence

Saints
surround me
with the secrets
of your stories

Little ones
challenge me
with the courage
of your living

Children
play with me,
pull me
towards heaven.

Ruth Burgess

Immersion

Incoming tide of God – cover my feet.
I yield the direction of my life to You.

Incoming tide of God – cover my knees
I yield the rule of my life to You.

Incoming tide of God – cover my hands.
I yield the shaping of my life to You.

Incoming tide of God – cover my heart.
I yield the tending of my emotions to You.

Incoming tide of God – cover my head.
I yield my need for control to You.

Incoming tide of God – overwhelm me.
Carry me out into Your unimaginable depths.

Pat Bennett

I say a prayer

I say a prayer
a prayer to God
my joy, my maker

I say a prayer
a prayer to Jesus
my friend, my redeemer

I say a prayer
a prayer to the Holy Spirit
my life, my disturber

I say a prayer
a prayer for all my living
make me loving
keep me holy.

Ruth Burgess

A blessing based on Psalm 139

The Lord, our God,
to whom night is as clear as day,
guide your feet as you go.

The Lord, our God, be with you when you sit and when you stand,
encompass you and lead you by the hand.

The Lord, our God,
who knows your path and the places where you rest,
be with you in your waiting,
be your good news for sharing,
and lead you in the way that is everlasting.

Ian Cowie

A solemn peace and justice blessing

God has called you to live in integrity and justice.
May you love mercy, act justly and walk humbly with God.
Amen

Jesus has shown you how to love your enemies and neighbours.
May you seek to be peacemakers and to live in God's light.
Amen

The Holy Spirit has comforted and disturbed you with God's peace.
May you be full of joy and courage all your nights and days.
Amen

May Almighty God bless you,
the Maker, the Redeemer and the Giver of Life.
Amen.

Ruth Burgess

All your being

Go in peace and in love.
Be filled, through all your being,
with the fullness of God.

Ian Cowie

A haiku journey blessing

Walk well your journey.
May God keep you and guide you
all your nights and days.

Ruth Burgess

Peace wherever you go

The God of peace
grant you peace.
His peace
whatever you do,
wherever you go.
Amen

Ian Cowie

Notes on prayers

1. 'Good neighbours' was first published in *Words for Today 2003: Notes for Daily Bible Reading*, © IBRA, Editor: Nicola Slee. ISBN 1 904 02403 3.

2. Line 11 in 'May we recognise' by Peter Millar, from the poem 'A place of hope', in *An Iona Prayer Book*, Canterbury Press, 1998. ISBN 1 853112 05 4.

3. 'Persevere' was first published in *Blessed Be Our Table*, Neil Paynter, Wild Goose Publications, 2003. ISBN 1 901557 72 3.

4. 'Our loveliness' was first published in *Words for Today 2003: Notes for daily Bible Reading*, © IBRA, Editor: Nicola Slee. ISBN 1 904 02403 3.

5. The prayers 'Why God?', 'With those who …', 'Jesus, stiller of storms', 'A solemn peace and justice blessing' were first published in *My Peace I Give to You*, a resource book for the Week of Christian Unity 2004, Churches Together in Britain and Ireland.

Workshops

A haiku prayer workshop

Optimum size – 10/15 people
Time required – 70/85 minutes

Haiku is a form
of poetry or prayer that
anyone can write.

For this workshop you will need:

✓ Pens and paper
✓ A flip chart
✓ Some traditional haiku poems and prayers
✓ Some modern examples of haiku prayers
✓ A copy of a thesaurus

(Examples of haiku can be found in many poetry anthologies and on websites. There are two modern haiku prayers in this book: *A haiku prayer of hurt* and *A haiku journey blessing*. You could also ask participants to bring their favourite haiku to the workshop.)

Workshop format

Introduction

- Introduce yourself to the group. Invite people to introduce themselves.
- Explain that the style of the workshop is participatory. Participants will be encouraged to share what they have written but do not have to do so.

- Outline the content of the workshop and ask the group if they have any questions.

History of haiku

Talk about the history of haiku and look at some traditional examples. (See Appendix 1).

Modern haiku

Look at some modern haiku prayers and poems (5-7 5 syllables).

Adding a 7-7 couplet

Invite the group to work in pairs and to add couplets (two lines, each of seven syllables) to any of the poems and prayers they have looked at.

Share your couplets

Invite each pair to share with the group the poem or prayer they chose and the couplet they have added.

Choose a theme

Decide, as a group, a theme/s for the prayers that you want to write, e.g. journey, Advent, evening, justice and peace. (It could be more than one theme.)

Fill a flip chart

Ask the group to fill a page of a flip chart with words relating to the theme/s they have chosen.

Look up two or three of the words in a thesaurus and see what alternatives are suggested.

Write your own haiku

Let people work together or alone to write their own haiku (5-7-5 or 5-7-5-7-7) based on the chosen theme/s.

Share your writing

Bring the group back together, and invite people to share what they have written and/or what they have enjoyed and discovered in the process.

Haiku workshop – Suggested time scale

ACTIVITIES	MINUTES
Introduction	5–10
History of haiku	5–10
Modern examples	5–10
Adding a 7-7 couplet	10
Share your couplets	5
Choose a theme	5
Fill a flip chart	5
Write your own haiku	20
Share your writing	10
TOTAL	75/85

An extension of this workshop might be to create a poster on which to display the group's work.

Bibliography

1) *The Green Book of Poetry*, edited by Ivo Mosley, first published 1993, Frontier Publishing, Norfolk, ISBN 1 872914 05 5.

2) http://inic.utexas.edu/asnic/countries/japan/haiku.html

Appendix 1

A short history of haiku

A haiku is a short poem or prayer composed of a fixed number of syllables. Haiku originated in Japan. An early anthology of poetry, the *Manyoshu*, collected around 630/760 A.D., includes short, lyrical poems, which some scholars believe were originally written as parts of ceremonial and religious rituals. The *Manyoshu* includes anonymous songs and prayers for safe journeys, planting and harvesting, courtship and marriage, as well as prayers to celebrate and pacify the gods.

Haiku has evolved and developed in form over the centuries. Most haiku consist of 17 syllables in a three-line 5-7-5 pattern. A 31-syllable haiku consisting of five lines in a three-line 5-7-5-7-7 pattern is sometimes used. At social gatherings in fourteenth-century Japan, a game developed where one person would compose the first part of the haiku (5-7-5), and others would add the two 7-syllable lines. The standard and subject matter of the verse sometimes reflected the amount of rice wine imbibed!

Matsuo Basho (1644–1694) was one of Japan's most celebrated haiku poets; Basho travelled widely within Japan and by the time of his death had more than two thousand students. While many of his poems lose their form in translation, they retain their clarity and directness:

By the road,
In the hedgerow, a rose –
My horse ate it.

Old pond –
Frog jumps in,
Sound of the water.[1]

Today, examples of haiku can be found in many poetry anthologies and in collections on the World Wide Web (see bibliography in *A Haiku Prayer Workshop*). Haiku is an accessible and disciplined poetic form, and a rewarding way in which to write short prayers.

[1] Both haiku translations © Ivo Mosley. From *A Green Book of Poetry*, edited by Ivo Mosley, first published 1993, Frontier Publishing, Norfolk, ISBN 1 872914 05 5.

A personal prayers workshop

Optimum size – 6/12 people
Time required – 70/90 minutes

For this workshop you will need:

✓ Pens and paper
✓ Scissors
✓ Prepared sheets ruled into boxes (see below) for each member of the group

Introduction

- Introduce yourself to the group. Invite people to introduce themselves.
- Explain that the style of the workshop is participatory, and that its process is about playfulness, experimentation and creativity. Participants will be encouraged to share what they have written but do not have to do so. Explain that there will be no pressure to produce a completed piece of writing.
- Outline the content of the workshop and ask the group if they have any questions.

Word association

Do some quick rounds of word association.

Suggested starter words: (choose 7 or 8, or be creative and use your own)

breakfast	story	wonder
Christmas	play	chocolate
church	Jesus	God
garden	fire	prayer
hope	hunger	courage

Sentence starters

Provide the group with a sentence starter (see below) and give them 5 minutes to write. They can write as little or as much as they choose within 5 minutes.

Repeat this process with the two additional sentence starters.

Suggested sentence starters (5 minutes each):

Today I feel …
I believe in a God who …
Sometimes I am surprised …

Mixing up

1. Invite each member of the group to choose words and phrases from what they have written that they'd like to respond to, or to think more about.

2. Write these words and phrases into boxes on a prepared sheet.

3. Cut out these individual boxes and play around with them, arranging them in different orders to get new and interesting ideas and phrases.

Writing your own prayer

Give members of the group 20/30 minutes to write by themselves. Invite people to develop any themes or ideas that have emerged from the workshop in whatever ways they choose.

Sharing

Bring the group back together, and invite people to share what they have written and/or what they have enjoyed and discovered in the process.

Personal prayers workshop – Suggested time scale

ACTIVITIES	MINUTES
Introduction	5/10
Word association	5
Sentence starters	15
Mixing up	15
Writing prayers	20/30
Sharing	10/15
TOTAL	70/90

Note:

I'm grateful to Yvonne Morland for sharing the process of this workshop with me. As with any process, it is open to addition, refinement and improvisation. We would welcome feedback, creative suggestions and additions.

A workshop on writing intercessory/bidding prayers

Maximum size – 20 people
Time required – 85/95 minutes

(This workshop could be divided into two sections. See *Suggested time scale* at the end of this section.)

Bidding prayers are also referred to as prayers of concern or intercessions. The word *bid* in Anglo-Saxon means *pray*.

For this workshop you will need:

✓ Pens and paper
✓ A flip chart
✓ A handout of *The pattern of intercessory/bidding prayers and some examples* (Appendix 2).
✓ A handout with the readings for a particular day – either lectionary readings or readings you have chosen on a particular theme.
✓ Copies of current local and national newspapers.
✓ A handout of *Some observations and the Do's and Don'ts of writing intercessory prayers* (Appendix 3).

Introduction

• Introduce yourself to the group. Invite participants to introduce themselves.
• Explain that the aims of the workshop are to look at one pattern of intercessory prayer and to write prayers relating to a particular theme.

- Explain that the pattern of prayer used in the workshop may not totally correspond with the patterns used in individual churches, but that much of its content is adaptable.
- Inform participants that part of the workshop will include reading what they have written, and suggest that they write only what they are comfortable sharing with the group.
- Outline the content of the workshop and ask the group if they have any questions.

Different styles of intercessory prayer

Invite the group to discuss the following:

- What name is used to describe the prayers of intercession used in your church? Some churches call them bidding prayers. Have you heard of any other names?
- Who writes the bidding prayers in your church?
- Who leads the bidding prayers in your church?
- Where does the person leading the prayers kneel or stand? Is there any reason for this? In some churches the person leading intercessory prayers stands in the middle of the congregation in order to emphasise that these prayers relate to the concerns of the congregation.
- Have you noticed any differences in the ways other churches organise bidding prayers?

Theme/lectionary readings

- Distribute a handout that contains the text of the lectionary readings for the day, or readings you have chosen relating to a particular theme. You may wish to concentrate on the Old Testament and the Gospel passages for the day, but you can also choose to include a Psalm and a New

Testament reading that enhance the theme.
- Ask volunteers to read the passages out loud.

What kind of God?

- Ask the group to underline, within the texts, words that are used to address/describe God. (Give 5 minutes to do this.)
- Write these words up on the flip chart.
- Suggest that these words, and the picture of God that they portray, can be used in the beginning and end of the prayer.

What's happening in the world?

Do this exercise in pairs.
- Give out copies of local and national papers (broad sheet and tabloid).
- Ask each pair to identify three concerns.
- Write the concerns up on the flip chart. (There may be some overlap.)

(This section can be shortened by providing headlines.)

The pattern of the prayer

1. Distribute a handout of *The pattern of intercessory/bidding prayers and some examples* (Appendix 2). You may wish to provide further examples from a variety of traditions.
2. Read through the section on the pattern of bidding prayers.
3. Look at the lectionary readings for Christmas Day.
4. Look at the pattern of the bidding prayer for Christmas Day:

   Call to prayer
   Prayer of global concern
   Response
   Prayer relating to the theme of the day
   Response

Prayer for families and communities

Response

Prayer for those who are sick and for those who have died

Response

Prayer for personal needs

Response

Ending of the prayer and an AMEN.

5. Discuss how the beginning (call) and ending of the prayer echo the chosen theme and readings.
6. Note the move from global to personal concerns.
7. Note that the biddings are broken up by punctuation, giving the reader spaces to breathe and the congregation spaces to reflect on each part of the prayer.
8. Ask the group which responses are regularly used in their churches. Suggest that, when writing new responses, the Psalms are a good resource.
9. Note that the prayers and responses are written in inclusive language.
10. Invite comments.

(Look at some other examples of prayers if you have time.)

Writing prayers in groups

Invite participants to work in groups of four, and to write bidding prayers relating to the theme/lectionary readings and world concerns that they discussed earlier.

Two people in the group could write the beginning and the ending of the prayer, while the other two write the biddings and response, or the group could divide the exercise another way.

Sharing your writing

- Invite each group to read aloud the prayers they have written.
- Talk about the process and what has been produced. Ask the group if there were particular parts of the process that they found difficult, disliked or enjoyed.
- Thank each group for their contribution.

Distribute the handout *Some observations and the Do's and Don'ts of writing intercessory prayers* (Appendix 3) and invite people either to read it whilst in the group or to take it home and read it later.

Intercessory/bidding prayer workshop – Suggested time scale

PART ONE

ACTIVITIES	MINUTES
Introduction	10
Different styles of intercessory prayer	10
Theme/lectionary readings	10
What kind of God?	10
What's happening in the world	5/15
TOTAL	45/55

and

PART TWO

ACTIVITIES	MINUTES
The pattern of the prayer	10/20
Writing prayers	20/30
Sharing what you've written	15
TOTAL	45/65

Or

ACTIVITIES	MINUTES
Introduction	10
Different styles of intercessory prayer	10
Theme/lectionary readings	10
What kind of God?	5
What's happening in the world?	5/15
The pattern of the prayer	10
Writing prayers in groups	20
Sharing what you've written	15
TOTAL	85/95

Appendix 2

The pattern of intercessory/ bidding prayers
– and some examples

The pattern of bidding prayers

- These prayers have a beginning/call to prayer and an ending, which in some traditions are spoken by the worship leader/priest. In between are biddings that focus on particular concerns.

- Often the prayer is broken up by spoken or sung responses.

- The usual pattern of the biddings is to start with the global, progress through the national to the local, and end with the personal.

- Prayers for those who are sick, and for those who are dying or who have recently died are traditionally included.

- The theme of the service and/or the lectionary readings for the day will suggest content for the beginning and ending of the bidding prayer.

(See overleaf for some examples of bidding prayers.)

Examples of bidding prayers

1. Bidding prayers – Christmas Day

(Lectionary readings: Isaiah 52:7–10; Psalm 97; Hebrews 1:1–6; John 1:1–18)

Worship Leader: In the beginning
                    You were
                    In this moment
                    You are
                    You are strength and weakness
                    You are light and glory
                    You are God, and You welcome us,
                    You listen for our prayers …

We pray today for peace, peace in Jerusalem, peace in the dark places of our world. We pray for leaders and negotiators, for peace makers and peace keepers, for fighters and for prisoners, for all who are caught up in conflict and war and fear … We pray for peace and justice.

God, in your mercy,   HEAR OUR PRAYER

We pray for children everywhere, for the newly born, for those growing up among us, for those growing up in places where there is hunger and danger and fear … We pray that they may be loved and welcomed … that they may know courage and smiles and joy …

God, in your mercy,   HEAR OUR PRAYER

We pray for all who sit and eat with us today. We thank you for our families, for our friends, for those who love us, for those who share our laughter and pain … We pray for those who by choice or by circumstance eat alone … We pray for justice for those who are hungry …

God, in your mercy,   HEAR OUR PRAYER

We pray for all who are sick, and for those who care for them and pray for them … We pray for those who have died, for those we miss at our table … Tell them how much we love them, how much we miss them … Tell them we carry their stories in our lives …

God, in your mercy,   HEAR OUR PRAYER

We pray for ourselves, for our needs, our concerns, our hopes and our dreams …

God, in your mercy,   HEAR OUR PRAYER

Worship leader: Bright loving God, Emmanuel, God-with-us,
                   help us to recognise You today,
                   and to welcome You into our lives,
                   in wonder, in truth, and in holy joy.   AMEN

2. Elements of prayers of intercession for a Harvest Sunday

God of goodness and justice,
You know what we want to tell you.
Come into our hearts and minds and help us to pray …

We pray for areas of the world where the earth is polluted and people are exploited … We pray for those who make decisions about the distribution and use of land … We pray for wisdom and justice.

God of Creation,   HEAR OUR PRAYER

We pray for those who live in rural areas, for those whose livelihoods are dependent on the weather and the harvest and on economic strategies ... We pray for a good harvest and for just laws ...

God of Creation,   HEAR OUR PRAYER

We pray for ourselves, that we may be good stewards of creation.

God of Creation,   HEAR OUR PRAYER

Loving and truthful God,
nurture us amongst the wheat and weeds of our world,
and bring us mature and full of goodness
to shine like the sun in Your golden harvest.

3. Elements of prayers for All Saints Day (written in Northumbria and referring to local saints)

God of love and mercy,
we, your children,
join with the saints to love and praise you,
and to bring you our prayers of concern ...

We pray for those whose stories we have heard on the news this week ... for those who are excited and joyful ... for those who are travelling ... for those who are hungry and fearful ... for those who are angry ... for those who are waiting ... for those who are sad ...

Holy God,   HOW HAPPY ARE THOSE WHO TRUST IN YOU

We give you thanks for the saints of Northumbria ... for the vision of Cuthbert and the wisdom of Hilda, for the patience and trust of Aidan, the poetry of Caedmon and the faithfulness of Bede. We thank you for their humanity, for their mistakes and their successes, for their love for you ...
Holy God,   HOW HAPPY ARE THOSE WHO TRUST IN YOU

We pray for ourselves ... We are your saints in this place. Dream your dreams in us, nurture our faith and our love.
Holy God,   HOW HAPPY ARE THOSE WHO TRUST IN YOU

Pilgrim God,
lead us homewards.
May your saints encourage us,
your angels guard us,
and your little ones dance with us along the way.

Appendix 3

Some observations and the

The Do's and Don'ts of writing intercessory prayers

Bidding prayers – some observations

- Bidding or intercessory prayers are the prayers that members of a congregation are most often asked to write and/or lead.
- These prayers arise out of a congregation's concerns, both global and local.
- There should be moments of silence within these prayers to allow spaces for the individual prayers and reflections (spoken or silent) of the congregation.
- Short bidding prayers enable individuals to focus on a topic; longer prayers can be confusing.
- Bidding prayers should not be prescriptive. They should not contain suggestions to God or the congregation as to appropriate ways to act!
  (E.g. We pray for those who are in trouble … that God may show them the error of their ways.)
- The use of a well known said or sung response, between sections of the prayer, helps people concentrate, and provides opportunity for the congregation to give verbal assent to the prayer. *(E.g. God in your mercy … HEAR OUR PRAYER.)*
- Bidding prayers should reflect both current concerns and the theme of the service. Where a lectionary is used, the readings for the day will suggest themes and concepts for the prayers. (For example, Christmas readings could lead into prayers relating to poverty, refugees or homelessness.)

Prayers about current events do not necessarily need to link in with the theme and/or readings.

- Bidding prayers can be written and/or led by more than one member of the congregation.
- Bidding prayers are often led by someone kneeling/standing in the midst of the congregation. If you intend to do this, ensure that the prayers are audible throughout the building.

The Do's and Don'ts of writing intercessory prayers

DON'T

✗ Have too many themes within one section/bidding.

✗ Use words or phrases that are difficult to pronounce.

✗ Write prescriptive prayers.

✗ Write prayers a long time before they are needed, unless you are able to add in recent concerns easily, at a later stage.

DO

✓ Read through the lectionary readings and think about the theme of the service before you write.

✓ Watch the news and read the papers before you write and be aware of local issues.

✓ Use a response familiar to the congregation – if you want to introduce a new response write the words on the service sheet.

✓ Write in short phrases and break up longer sentences with punctuation.

✓ Read out loud the prayers you have written to ensure that they will be easy to read in a service.

✓ Use phrases and concepts from the Bible readings within the opening and closing parts of the prayer.

✓ Use inclusive language, particularly in responses.

✓ Indicate spaces for silence/reflection within the prayer.

✓ Write the prayers with someone else if you prefer to do so.

✓ Keep copies of what you have written for future reference.

✓ Share your skills with others – the more people involved in writing prayers the better!

Contributors

Alison Adam works freelance, resourcing churches and organisations in liturgy and song. She is a member of the Iona Community.

Anon prefers to remain anonymous in case his/her visitors never return.

Jenny and John Ayre 'are ecumenical nomads who find God by the estuary with Him calling through the curlew'. They have spent time on Lindisfarne and seek God in creation.

Elizabeth Baxter is joint Executive Director of Holy Rood House, Centre for Health and Pastoral Care, in Thirsk, North Yorkshire, and the Centre for the Study of Theology and Health. As a priest and counsellor, she accompanies people on their therapeutic and spiritual journeys. Her liturgy springs from these experiences.

Benjamin and Michelle, who are now adults, wrote their prayers that appear in this book when they were children in school.

Pat Bennett is an associate member of the Iona Community. She has been writing prayers, liturgies, hymns and songs since her first visit to Iona in 1996.

Jan Berry is a minister of the United Reformed Church and Tutor in Practical Theology at Northern College, Manchester (part of the Partnership for Theological Education). She has a particular interest in feminist liturgy and ritual.

Deb Buckley lives in Birmingham where she works as a part-time counsellor. She is passionate about issues of justice and spends much of her time co-running a fair trade business.

Nick Burden lives in Newcastle upon Tyne and worships at St Gabriel's Church, Heaton. He is an associate of the Iona Community.

Ruth Burgess is a writer and editor. She is currently working part-time with the Alzheimer's Society, supporting people with dementia. She lives in the north east of England, likes fireworks and growing flowers and food. She is a member of the Iona Community.

Joyce Clarke died in 2001. She was a minister and lived in Macclesfield in England. 'Most of my prayers are my "conversations" with God during wakeful nights.' She is also published in *A Book of Blessings* (Wild Goose Publications).

David Coleman spends his time as parent to Taliesin and Melangell, partner to Zam, and as a minister with Barrhead United Reformed Church. He is longing to see the birth of the united free catholic church, but for now works energetically and ecumenically where he can. He is investigating how a more audio-visual approach can enrich the worship of a local church. He is a member of the Iona Community.

Frances Copsey – 'I find having MS a full-time job these days, but go on searching for meaning and love among both friends and strangers (there's a lot of it about). Exploring reality through language gives me great pleasure.'

Ian Cowie is a retired Church of Scotland minister. Most recently he was chaplain to the Christian Fellowship of Healing (Scotland), a drop in centre where folk could find help without the trappings of a church. His books include *People Praying, Growing Knowing Jesus, Across the Spectrum, Prayers and Ideas for Healing Services* (Wild Goose Publications), and *Jesus' Healing Works and Ours* (Wild Goose Publications). He is married and has five children and seven grandchildren.

Andrew Foster is an engineer living in Ontario, Canada, a regular visitor to Iona, and a friend of the Iona Community. He is an elder in the Presbyterian Church in Canada, and enjoys writing.

Ian M. Fraser has three children and nine grandchildren. He and his wife, Margaret, who died in 1987, served Rosyth Parish Church, Scottish Churches' House, the World Council of Churches, and the Department of Mission in Selly Oak Colleges.

Jenni Sophia Fuchs was born in Germany, but grew up in Edinburgh, which she now calls home. She holds degrees in Scottish Ethnology and Museum Studies. She has lived and worked in England, Wales, the United States, and on the Isle of Iona, where she did various stints as children's worker for the Iona Community. She has been an associate member of the Iona Community since 1998.

Kathy Galloway is the current Leader of the Iona Community. She is the author/editor of several books including *Dreaming of Eden, Pushing the Boat Out, Starting Where We Are, The Pattern of Our Days* and *Praying for the Dawn* (with Ruth Burgess), all published by Wild Goose Publications.

Louise Glen-Lee needs more time, has 1 husband, 2 children, 1 dog, 1 job at the Salvation Army Soup Kitchen. She wishes for world peace, and desires 24 hour shopping (when workers are paid fairly and there are always large sizes left).

Tom Gordon is a hospice chaplain with Marie Curie Cancer Care in Edinburgh. He is the author of *A Need for Living* (Wild Goose Publications), a speaker, facilitator and writer on spiritual care, death and dying, and bereavement.

Liz Gregory-Smith is a retired teacher, a wife, and a mother of two adult sons.

Hackwood Park School is a school for children with moderate learning difficulties situated near Hexham, Northumberland. Children aged 9–16 years worked with Lindsay Gray to produce the prayers in this book. The children are Amanda, Anne Marie, Ashley, Carl, Chris, Christopher, Christopher, Darren, Deborah, Diane, Ellen, Emma, Gary, Gav, James, Jason, Jay, John, Josh, Martyn, Matthew, Paul, Simon.

Margaret Harvey is a founder member of the Coleg y Groes Community and helps to run the Coleg y Groes Retreat House in Corwen, North Wales. She is a native of Wales and a Church in Wales priest.

Pam Hathorn has been senior special needs teacher in a large comprehensive school in Berkshire for many years.

Annie Heppenstall-West is a mural painter, writer, supply teacher, and mum. She lives in Yorkshire with her husband and son. She is the author of *Reclaiming the Sealskin: Meditations in the Celtic Spirit* (Wild Goose Publications).

Jim Hughes is a member of the Iona Community. He has spent most of his working life in industry and university teaching.

Kate McIlhagga was a minister, latterly in Northumberland, involved in writing, retreat work and the local hospice until she died in 2002. She was a member of the Iona Community and of its area of concern exploring spirituality.

Joy Mead is a member of the Iona Community. She works freelance as poet, writer and editor and leads small creative writing groups. For many years she has been involved in development education and justice and peace work. Poetry is a main interest and her poems have been included in many magazines and anthologies. She is author/editor of *Compassion in the Market Place*, *The One Loaf* and *A Telling Place*, all published by Wild Goose Publications.

Michelle (*see* Benjamin and Michelle)

Rosie Miles lives in Birmingham and lectures in English at the University of Wolverhampton. She has also contributed to *Praying for the Dawn* (1999) and *A Book of Blessings* (2001), both published by Wild Goose Publications.

Yvonne Morland is a poet and writer with a passion for liturgical exploration. She has been writing for Wild Goose Publications since 1995 and has been a full member of the Iona Community since August 2002. She is about to engage in a more sustained piece of writing, exploring the importance of vulnerability in human exchange, which she hopes will appear in published form sometime in 2005.

Rosie G. Morton worked as a nurse, mainly in the areas of cancer and palliative care, before beginning training for ordained Anglican ministry at Queen's College, Birmingham. She has a variety of interests which include hill walking, spirituality and the arts, writing poems and prayers, and spending time with friends and family.

Ivo Mosley studied Japanese at Oxford University. He spent seventeen years as a professional ceramist before turning full-time writer. His work includes musicals, fiction, poetry, and books on culture, politics and society.

Jean Murdoch died in spring 2003. She lived in Oban and was an associate member of the Iona Community. She is also published in *A Book of Blessings* (Wild Goose Publications).

da Noust is a pen name for the creative activities of members and friends of L'Arche Edinburgh, a community welcoming adults with learning disabilities to a life shared with assistants and others whose time and energy is a gift. The four prayers in this book have musical settings: for example, 'Persevere' uses Mayenziwe (traditional South African melody), and 'Saviour of all pilgrim people' takes the carol 'Quem Pastores'.

Neil Paynter has worked in homeless shelters, nursing homes, and as a writer and editor. His collections include *Lent & Easter Readings from Iona* (Wild Goose Publications), *This Is the Day* (Wild Goose Publications), and *Blessed Be Our Table: Graces for Mealtimes & Reflections on Food* (Wild Goose Publications). He occasionally does gigs as a stand-up comedian.

Jan Sutch Pickard is a writer, storyteller, and the current Warden of Iona Abbey. 'Iona is a good place to make friends from all over the world,' she writes. Her prayers reflect life in community.

Chris Polhill was one of the first women to be ordained priest in the Church of England, and in 2004 celebrates 10 years as a priest and 20 years in ministry. She serves in the Lichfield diocese in three parishes, and on a project linking the environment and spirituality.

Jocelyn Prosser is a visual artist with work in private collections in Toronto and London. Her painting 'Urban Spirit' features on the cover of Friends and Enemies. She writes: 'Painting gives me release from the many problems I have encountered ... I hope that my work will always be from the heart.' Jocelyn Prosser was born in Toronto, Canada, and now lives in South Wales with her husband and two children. www.artnaive.co.uk

Karen Reeves-Attwood is a member of the Iona Community and co-convenor of the Racism Matters working group. She has worked in community health over a number of years, and is currently training for ordained ministry in the Church of England.

Norman Shanks was Leader of the Iona Community from 1995–2002 and is now minister of Govan Old Parish Church in Glasgow.

Nicola Slee is a theologian and poet based at the Queen's Foundation, Birmingham. She has been published widely, including poems and prayers in a number of Wild Goose anthologies. Her introduction to Christian feminist theology, Faith and Feminism, is published by DLT, and a collection of her prayers and poems entitled Praying Like a Woman is shortly to be published by SPCK.

Mary Taylor has an MA in Creative Writing and has had poems published in many magazines. She also performs her work in a wide range of venues and runs workshops. She contributes to Sanctuary, an alternative worship group, for which 'In your work' was written.

Simon Taylor is a Baptist minister, currently serving as County Ecumenical Officer for Devon. He lives on Dartmoor and is involved in the St Michael's (Princetown) Trust, which aims to communicate care for creation, particularly through the experience of wonder.

Cath Threlfall works for a local charity that supports adults and young people who have severe learning and physical disabilities. She is married and has three grown-up sons and an eleven-year-old daughter.

Tobermory High School is on the Isle of Mull in Scotland. Children from the high school worked with Jan Sutch Pickard to produce prayers for a Christmas service. The children are Callum, Charlotte, Douglas, Holly.

Gerke van Hiele is a minister in an open and ecumenical community in Holland. He is an associate of the Iona Community, and one of the initiators of the Dutch Iona Group. Together with Teun Kruijswijk Jansen, he edited the Dutch and English song and prayer book *Liederen en Gebeden from Iona & Glasgow* (Kok, 2003).

Zam Walker Coleman has been busy this year. In addition to being a parent to Taliesin (4) and Melangell (2), she has been exploring the spirituality of cancer in both theory and practice. Other passions are issues of gender and sexuality. She particularly hopes that the Church will celebrate God's wonderful diversity in creation and become fully inclusive. She is a member of the Iona Community.

Jean Williams is a member of the Iona Community and runs workshops on 'Celtic Spirituality'.

Lynda Wright is a member of the Iona Community. In the past she worked in parish ministry, and on Iona as a member of the resident group. She now lives in Falkland, Scotland at Key House, which is a place of welcome and hospitality offering quiet space for reflection and rest.

Index of authors

The Iona Community

The Iona Community, founded in 1938 by the Revd George MacLeod, then a parish minister in Glasgow, is an ecumenical Christian community committed to seeking new ways of living the Gospel in today's world. Initially working to restore part of the medieval abbey on Iona, the Community today remains committed to 'rebuilding the common life' through working for social and political change, striving for the renewal of the church with an ecumenical emphasis, and exploring new, more inclusive approaches to worship, all based on an integrated understanding of spirituality.

The Community now has over 240 Members, about 1500 Associate Members and around 1500 Friends. The Members – women and men from many denominations and backgrounds (lay and ordained), living throughout Britain with a few overseas – are committed to a fivefold Rule of devotional discipline, sharing and accounting for use of time and money, regular meeting, and action for justice and peace.

At the Community's three residential centres – the Abbey and the MacLeod Centre on Iona, and Camas Adventure Camp on the Ross of Mull – guests are welcomed from March to October and over Christmas. Hospitality is provided for over 110 people, along with a unique opportunity, usually through week-long programmes, to extend horizons and forge relationships through sharing an experience of the common life in worship, work, discussion and relaxation. The Community's shop on Iona, just outside the Abbey grounds, carries an attractive range of books and craft goods.

The Community's administrative headquarters are in Glasgow, which also serves as a base for its work with young people, the Wild Goose Resource Group working in the field of worship, a bi-monthly magazine, *Coracle*, and a publishing house, Wild Goose Publications.

For information on the Iona Community contact:
The Iona Community, Fourth Floor, Savoy House, 140 Sauchiehall Street,
Glasgow G2 3DH, UK. Phone: 0141 332 6343
e-mail: ionacomm@gla.iona.org.uk; web: www.iona.org.uk

For enquiries about visiting Iona, please contact:
Iona Abbey, Isle of Iona, Argyll PA76 6SN, UK. Phone: 01681 700404
e-mail: ionacomm@iona.org.uk

Also from Wild Goose Publications ...

A Book of Blessings
... and how to write your own
Ruth Burgess

From the author of *Friends and Enemies,* this Wild Goose best-seller is a collection of blessings for the people, sadnesses, artefacts, special occasions and journeys of our lives. It also explores the tradition of blessings, including biblical and Celtic, and offers ideas and resources to encourage readers to write blessings of their own, with suggestions for how to organise a blessings workshop.

ISBN 1 901557 48 0

Praying for the Dawn
A resource book for the ministry of healing
Ruth Burgess & Kathy Galloway

A compilation of material from several writers with strong emphasis on liturgies and resources for healing services. Includes a section on how to introduce healing services to those who may not be familiar with them, and suggestions for starting group discussions about healing. The book is rounded off by a section of worship resources – prayers, responses, litanies, poems, meditations and blessings.

ISBN 1 901557 26 X

Go to www.ionabooks.com for full details of all our publications and online ordering

Cherish the Earth
Reflections on a living planet
Mary Low

A fine collection of readings, poems, theology and liturgy to help us start rethinking our beliefs as if the rest of nature mattered. Among the poets and authors featured are Chinua Achebe, Alan Spence, Ted Hughes, W.H. Davies, Eunice Buchanan, Waldo Williams, John Agard, Kathleen Raine, R.S. Thomas, Satish Kumar, Chaim Potok, Betsy White, Barbara Kingsolver, Leo Tolstoy, Adomnán of Iona, Jonathon Porritt, Albert Schweitzer, Pierre Teilhard de Chardin and others.

ISBN 1 901557 71 5

This Is the Day
Readings and meditations from the Iona Community
Neil Paynter

Daily readings for four months from a wide range of contributors within the Iona Community. These prayers, liturgies, songs, poems and articles, which reflect the concerns of the Community, can be used for group or individual reflection and are intended to inspire positive action and change in our lives.

ISBN 1 901557 63 4

Out of Iona
Words from a crossroads of the world
Jan Sutch Pickard

Iona Abbey Warden Jan Sutch Pickard follows her best-selling *Dandelions & Thistles* with this new collection of her poems, readings and reflections which capture not only the wildness and beauty of Iona but also the pressures and gifts of living in a community on an island of pilgrimage. Includes a large section of biblical reflections.

ISBN 1 901557 77 4

Wild Goose Publications, the publishing house of the Iona Community established in the Celtic Christian tradition of Saint Columba, produces books, tapes and CDs on:

- holistic spirituality
- social justice
- political and peace issues
- healing
- innovative approaches to worship
- song in worship, including the work of the Wild Goose Resource Group
- material for meditation and reflection

If you would like to find out more about our books, tapes and CDs, please contact us at:

Wild Goose Publications
Fourth Floor, Savoy House
140 Sauchiehall Street,
Glasgow G2 3DH, UK

Tel. +44 (0)141 332 6292
Fax +44 (0)141 332 1090
e-mail: admin@ionabooks.com

or visit our website at
www.ionabooks.com
for details of all our products and online sales